Dick Francis

STEEPLECHASE JOCKEY

Also by Bryony Fuller

TOM DREAPER AND HIS HORSES
FULKE WALWYN – A PICTORIAL TRIBUTE
VINCENT O'BRIEN – THE NATIONAL HUNT YEARS

Dick Francis

STEEPLECHASE JOCKEY

by Bryony Fuller

FOREWORD BY PETER O'SULLEVAN

MICHAEL JOSEPH
LONDON

MICHAEL JOSEPH LTD

Published by the Penguin Group
27 Wrights Lane, London W8 5TZ
Viking Penguin Inc., 375 Hudson Street, New York, New York 10014, USA
Penguin Books Australia Ltd, Ringwood, Victoria, Australia
Penguin Books Canada Ltd, 10 Alcorn Avenue, Toronto, Ontario, Canada M4V 3B2
Penguin Books (NZ) Ltd, 182–190 Wairau Road, Auckland 10, New Zealand

Penguin Books Ltd, Registered Offices: Harmondsworth, Middlesex, England

First published in Great Britain, September 1994
Second impression November 1994

Copyright © Bryony Fuller 1994

Typeset by Selwood Systems, Midsomer Norton
Printed in Great Britain by Butler & Tanner Ltd, Frome and London

ISBN 0 7181 3811 2

The moral right of the author has been asserted

Contents

Author's Acknowledgements

THIS BOOK WOULD NOT HAVE BEEN POSSIBLE without the enormous help and co-operation of Dick Francis and his elder brother Doug; both their wives, Mary and Julia, were also most kind and helpful. I must also thank Dick's two sons, Merrick and Felix, for their help and encouragement, and for lending me so many family photographs.

The Hon. Dr Honor Vivian Smith provided invaluable information about her father, the first Lord Bicester, and his affiliation with Dick when he rode for him; Ken Cundell also was very informative about Dick's riding days for both himself and his cousin Frank. Aubrey Brabazon, a contemporary of Dick's, was as always helpful and amusing. I must also thank another great jockey of that era, Martin Maloney.

I am very grateful to Peter O'Sullevan and Sir Edward Cazalet for generously contributing the Foreword and Preface respectively, and to Edward especially for the loan of much material relating to Dick's time as stable jockey at Fairlawne. Tim Cox, as always, did great work on the statistics. Finally, I should like to thank my editors Jenny Dereham and Rory Smith for their patience and interest.

The following I should also like to thank for their time and help:

Toby Balding	Dickie Onslow
Harry Beeby	George Owen
Bunny Cooper	Jane Owen
Peter Cundell	Charmian Powell
Jack Garland	Susan Purcell
Reg Green	John Randall
The late Sir Martin Gilliat	Bill Rees
Brenda Kilford	Irene Rixson
Sir Rupert Mackeson	Cath Walwyn
Lady Mary Mundford	John Welcome
Diana Nicholson	The Clerks of the Courses
Lavinia, Duchess of	of Aintree, Chepstow,
Norfolk	Cheltenham and
Dr Vincent O'Brien	Kempton racecourses

Foreword

BY PETER O'SULLEVAN

IF MODESTY IS A HALLMARK of the outstanding sportsman, Dick Francis, champion jump jockey of 1954 and one of the outstanding horsemen of his era, has it in abundance. Dick was a very young man when the renowned horsemaster and successful trainer Tom Masson, who was directing the Bertram Mills circus troupe at the time, observed, 'A better pair of hands on a pony I have yet to see.' Who could have foretold that more than a quarter of a century later the sensitive hands which guided 345 winners as well as the most cataclysmic loser in the history of National Hunt racing would be tapping a two-fingered tattoo to global literary fame?

'Our hero' – as Sir Martin Gilliat, longtime PPS to Queen Elizabeth The Queen Mother, always referred to Dick – achieved his first treble on 23 April 1949 at Bangor where his three rides during the afternoon, Mass, Rompworthy and Tommy Thrush, won by an aggregate of ten lengths. The middle 'leg' was trained by his equally self-effacing and charming brother Doug.

Eight years on, when sitting down to write his autobiography, *The Sport of Queens*, he signalled the most significant three-timer of an outstandingly successful career. Eighteenth-century clergyman and author Charles Colton wrote that there are three difficulties in authorship: 'To write anything worth publishing, to find honest men to publish it and to get sensible men to read it.' If all trebles were realised with such verve there would be very few bookmakers around.

Among the author's Acknowledgements which preface *The Sport of Queens* (published in hardback 2/12/57 price 21/–!) there is an expression of sincere and permanent gratitude, 'To my neighbour, Geoffrey Boumphrey, author and inventor, for the lessons I learned from his lucid prose and style'. A man of diverse talents, the late Geoffrey Boumphrey regularly presented the BBC TV programme *Inventors' Club* in the late 1950s and early 1960s as well as writing popular children's stories and editing books such as *The Shell Guide to Britain* which featured some of his own scholarly essays. Geoffrey had a great facility for communicating his knowledge and erudition, and Dick recently recalled: 'I learned so much from him that was absolutely priceless when it came to writing, not only *The Sport of Queens*, but the future Dick Francis books as well.'

The closing words of the original edition of Dick's autobiography read: 'I heard one man say to another, a little while ago, "Who did you say that was? Dick Francis? Oh, yes, he's the man who didn't win the National." What an epitaph!'

Happily, to the delight of millions the world over, Dick Francis has been rewriting that epitaph for the past thirty-six years. And, hopefully, will continue to do so for many years to come.

Peter O'Sullevan

Preface

BY SIR EDWARD CAZALET

Across the world most people will tell you that Dick Francis is one of the greatest thriller writers of all time. Yet by the middle of the 1950s, before he had written a single piece for publication, his was a household name as a champion steeplechase jockey. What a double!

I first met Dick in the early 1950s. He had taken only a few years to reach the top as a professional steeplechase jockey. It was in March 1953 that he came to see my father, Peter Cazalet, to be interviewed for the job of first jockey at Fairlawne. On the same day, my father, who had the living rights of our local parish, was to interview a new vicar. When Dick arrived for his interview, so the story goes, his charming manner was so much more like that of a parson than a jockey that my father spent a quarter of an hour discussing hymns and the length of sermons before Dick was able, politely, to point out the mistake.

I was lucky enough to know Dick and Mary well. Over three very happy and successful seasons Dick rode for my father's stable. In the 1953/54 season he rode winner after winner and was leading jockey. He was a natural and superb horseman, his skill having been learnt in the hunting field and show ring rather than on the racecourse. No one can become a champion without being an effective finisher, but Dick's skills were based on balance and security – the ability to get horses jumping and to stay on board when, for whatever reason, they made appalling blunders. As you look at this superb collection of photographs, the first thing you notice is the length of his leathers in contrast with the Piggott style of today's jump jockeys. You also notice how well-balanced and relaxed his mounts almost invariably were.

Fred Winter, from whom Dick took the Championship, remembers him as 'very competitive but the best loser I ever rode against. He gave nothing away in a race but was always the first to come up afterwards and say "Well done" if you happened to come off best.'

One thing I particularly remember about Dick was that whenever he came to ride schooling he always had the common sense to wear a crash helmet. I know of no other jockey who did this until more than a decade later, well on into the 1960s, in fact.

The fall on the flat of Devon Loch when twenty lengths in front and only fifty yards from the winning post in the 1956 Grand National seemed at the time to have been just about the worst luck that any jockey could suffer; but had it not happened Dick might well not have been asked to write his autobiography. A literary agent offered him a ghost writer, but Dick said that he would have a go himself. His autobiography *The Sport of Queens* showed him not only that writing was fun but also that he could write extremely well.

Just how well has been made consistently clear over the past thirty years – so it may well be that Devon Loch lit that literary spark which has since burned so brightly across the globe.

Now, nearly forty years on and more than thirty bestsellers later, Dick is still one of the most unpretentious, unassuming and enormously generous characters I know. Perhaps the most remarkable thing about both him and Mary is that Dick's complete success in two totally different fields has changed neither of them from being the delightful individuals that they have always been.

I recommend without reserve this wonderful book of Dick Francis in action, flirting with danger in a style to match the bravest of his fictional heroes. It also shows another side of a great and versatile craftsman.

Edward Cazalet

CHAPTER 1

Bred for the Game

Although modern racegoers may find it surprising that two of the most popular Champion National Hunt Jockeys of this century should hail from the small town of Tenby in Pembrokeshire, this would not have seemed strange to racegoers between the two world wars. In 1920 there was a thriving National Hunt circuit in south and west Wales and racing was held not only at Tenby, but also at Cardiff, Cowbridge, Monmouth and Newport, with Chepstow joining the circuit in 1926.

The first Champion Jockey for which Tenby was responsible was Dick Rees who was probably the best jump jockey up until the Second World War. He was five times Champion Jockey, and won all of jumping's classics – the Grand National, the Cheltenham Gold Cup, the Champion Hurdle and the Grand Steeplechase de Paris (the French Grand National). Dick Rees was to share many attributes and characteristics with our hero, Dick Francis. Firstly they were both known as Dick, although Rees was christened Fred Brychan and Francis, Richard Stanley. Both were born in or near Tenby and started their riding careers as amateurs in point-to-points: each served their country gallantly in the air, Dick Rees in the Royal Flying Corps (as the Royal Air Force was then known) during the First World War and Dick Francis in the Royal Air Force during the Second World War. Both were natural horsemen and particularly fine Aintree jockeys.

Dick Francis was born on 31 October 1920, the second son of Vincent and Molly Francis. His elder brother Doug (William Douglas) undoubtedly encouraged Dick to go into racing and it was largely thanks to Doug's efforts that after the Second World War Dick eventually made the breakthrough and became a working jockey. Doug and Dick remain the closest of friends today and it is due to Doug's generosity that I have been able to garner so much information about his famous younger brother. As everyone in racing knows, Dick is so modest

DICK AT SIX MONTHS

DICK WHEN TWO YEARS OLD, TAKEN IN
JANUARY 1923

about his career as a jockey that this ability is often overlooked.

History suggests that heredity plays a part in the production of champion jockeys. Lester Piggott's career speaks for itself. Lester's father, Keith, was a first-rate jump jockey and went on to train a Grand National winner with Ayala in 1963, while Ernie Piggott, his paternal grandfather, was also a champion jump jockey and won the Grand National twice. Another example of three generations of top-class National Hunt riders are the famous Irish racing family, the Beasleys, who for eighty years had members winning races at Punchestown, Cheltenham and

Liverpool. Bobby, a third generation champion, will be remembered by many as the winner of the 1961 Grand National on Nicolaus Silver and the 1974 Gold Cup on Captain Christy.

Peter Scudamore, who was Champion National Hunt Jockey seven times, was also bred for the game as his father, Michael, was an excellent jump jockey in the 1950s. Three of the highlights of Michael's impressive career were winning the 1957 Gold Cup on Linwell, the 1959 Grand National on Oxo, and riding Crudwell to his record fiftieth win in 1960.

In Dick Francis's case we can trace the family interest in hunting and racing back two generations for Willie Francis, Dick's grandfather, and his elder half-brother Robert Harries, were leading amateur riders in the south-west of Wales between 1883 and 1905. Robert Harries was more successful than Willie and came to be known as 'The Fred Archer of Wales'. Certainly he had a very impressive record at Tenby, riding there over a period of ten years. Out of a total of thirty-five rides he was only unplaced on six occasions. Some sixty or seventy years later, his great-half-nephew Dick Francis also established an incredible record at another small racecourse near the sea, Cartmel.

Dick's father, Vincent, decided at an early age to make horses his living in preference to farming like the rest of his family. When he was in his teens, in 1908, he went to ride for Colonel Lort-Phillips of Lawrenny Castle near Tenby. Lort-Phillips had for some time run one of the best National Hunt stables in the whole of the British Isles, his main patron being the Liverpudlian tycoon, Frank Bibby, for whom he won the Grand National in 1905 with Kirkland. As was common earlier this century, the trainer's licence was held by the stable's head lad, in this case E. Thomas, and it was not until the early years of this century when the Hon. George Lambton went to train for Lord Derby, that training became considered a suitable occupation for 'a gentleman'. The Lawrenny stables were run along the grandest lines. The then Champion Jockey, 'Titch' Frank Mason, was retained, only the best horses were purchased and no expense was spared. Some forty-five years later, Dick was to be employed as top jockey to a very similar establishment when he was retained as first jockey by the Royal trainer, Peter Cazalet, at Fairlawne in Kent.

Vincent Francis rode a number of winners in the years leading up to the outbreak of the First World War, but all the best rides from the

DICK'S FATHER, VINCENT FRANCIS, ON MOUNT ROYAL AT THE
INTERNATIONAL HORSE SHOW, OLYMPIA (1939)

MOLLY FRANCIS, DICK'S MOTHER, A VERY ELEGANT HORSEWOMAN

Lort-Phillips' stable went to Titch Mason. Titch was a very tough and able jockey, built on rather the same lines as Gordon Richards, Champion Jockey on the Flat an amazing twenty-six times. Mason and Richards each had a very upright stance, both while walking and mounted, and had remarkably short legs comparative to their body height.

In 1914, Vincent joined up for the duration of the First World War, and the following year he married; Douglas, the elder of his two sons, was born in 1916. When he was demobilised in 1918 as a Captain, Vincent considered his future carefully and came to the conclusion that the risk versus reward ratio involved in riding as second jockey for Lort-Phillips was unattractive with a wife and child, so instead he went to work as a nagsman for various Midlands hunt dealers.

CHAPTER 2

Schoolin', Showin' and Huntin'

There is no doubt that from a very early age Dick had an affinity with horses and, like most children, was particularly fond of the foals. He was born on Coedcanlas Farm in Pembrokeshire which belonged to his maternal grandparents, Willie and Molly Thomas. The farm ran down to the River Cleddeau and was virtually next door to the Rees brothers' farm. As Willie Thomas was a keen hunting man, there were always horses and ponies around the farm.

Doug and Dick were not given any formal riding lessons but rode on donkeys, ponies and horses from the time they could walk. Both brothers spent a great deal of their childhood at Coedcanlas, Douglas because of ill-health which he suffered until his early teens, and Dick during the school holidays as his grandmother always liked to have one or more of her children and grandchildren around. When Dick was aged ten his grandfather died and he then spent a year at the farm, ostensibly to keep his grandmother company. During this time he attended the local school, frequently riding there on his pony; in common with most horse-mad young boys, he considered school a tiresome waste of time.

From an early age, the Francis brothers did not play Cowboys and Indians or drive an imaginary Flying Scotsman. Their role models were the Rees brothers – Dick and Bilbie – who were then at the height of their careers: between them in the 1920s, they won two Grand Nationals, three Cheltenham Gold Cups and two Champion Hurdles. Doug and Dick were always horse mad and names such as Valentine's, Becher's and the Canal Turn were familiar to them from a very early age. In fact, Dick cannot recall a time when he did not want to be a jockey. Similarly, Felix, Dick's younger son, told me that one of the games he and his brother Merrick enjoyed playing with their father when they were little was 'riding the finish of the Grand National'. This consisted of each child sitting astride an arm of the sofa pretending they were coming into the last fence and storming away to win. Felix considered this a perfectly normal game to play as racing was, and still is, an important part of the Francis's family life. He was quite surprised when I mentioned that not all children practise riding races as a normal game.

Currently Dick is internationally known as one of the most successful thriller writers of the twentieth century. However, few of the millions of his fans probably know that as far as riding is concerned he was reckoned to be a child prodigy. By the age of five or six, not only was Dick extremely fond of horses and ponies but, more importantly, he was determined and eager to learn the finer points of riding. Even at this early age, when asked what he wanted to be when he was grown up, his reply was always 'to be a jockey'.

Around this time Dick's father became the manager of W.J. Smith's establishment near Maidenhead. Horace Smith was one of the

A RARE EARLY PHOTOGRAPH OF MARIA AND WILLIAM FRANCIS,
DICK'S GRANDPARENTS

largest dealers in quality hunters, hacks and children's ponies in the south of England. Because of their father's job, Doug and Dick had more opportunity to ride and school all sorts of horses and ponies than most boys of their age. Horace Smith also had a well-known riding school in Cadogan Place in London and it was on ponies that the young Francis brothers helped to school that HM The Queen and HRH Princess Margaret learned to ride.

By the age of seven, Dick was regularly going out hunting on a pony called Mickey. The next year he started to do well in showing classes on show ponies and in gymkhana events, and for some seven to eight years Dick was a leading rider in the show ring. The ponies which he rode usually belonged to either Horace Smith or Bertram Mills, the owner of the famous circus. Before founding his circus, Bertram Mills had been an undertaker, and by the time Dick started riding for him he was in his sixties and completely bald. Not only was he a very successful man but he was charismatic too and Dick has nothing but the fondest memories of him.

Dick never misses an opportunity to tell the story of how one day when he had been staying with Bertram Mills at Chalfont St Giles, he did not have enough money for his fare home. Without hesitation Bertram gave him a crispy, white five pound note – a fortune in the 1930s. In his book *The Sport of Queens* Dick relates how he got home free by tendering the note to

IN THE YARD AT EMBROOK HOUSE. FROM THE LEFT: DOUG FRANCIS,
DUDLEY SIMMS (A FAMILY FRIEND), VINCENT FRANCIS AND DICK

DICK AT A MEET OF THE GARTH HUNT AT
TOUCHEN END, A VILLAGE BETWEEN HOLY-
PORT AND HAWTHORN HILL, ON A HORSE
FROM W. J. SMITH'S HUNTING STABLES AT
HOLYPORT

DICK CHECKS HIS WATCH BEFORE GOING
HUNTING. HE WAS ALWAYS IMMACULATELY
DRESSED

DICK ON MIGNONETTE AFTER WINNING A CLASS AT HENLEY-ON-THAMES
IN 1934

bus conductors along the way who invariably did not have enough change. In those days it was possible to travel free if you did not have the correct fare – somewhat different from nowadays when you would probably be thrown off the bus.

Dick was very successful at showing ponies in junior show jumping. This was helped by the fact that until he was about fourteen he was tiny and didn't weigh much more than 5 stone. This lack of stature was a great advantage when showing ponies in the ring, but it was also a problem as his determination to be a jockey was always strong and he continually begged his parents to let him go into racing.

Dick told me that the first racehorse he ever rode was trained by David Harrison near Tenby. 'When I was aged from about twelve onwards, and staying with my grandmother at Coedcanlas to keep her company, we used to ride out on the beach early in the morning. Of course, the horses they put me on were very *easy* racehorses.'

DICK AND PADDY GALLAGHER, THE STUD GROOM, IN THE YARD AT EMBROOK HOUSE

DICK WITH HIS DOG, PETER

In those days, boys went off to be apprenticed for the Flat around the age of twelve, but despite Dick's continual pleas his parents were against the idea of their small son leaving home to go into such a tough and restrictive life. Suddenly he started to grow and by the time he was sixteen he had grown too big for the Flat; however, he still wasn't big or strong enough to be accepted as a trainee amateur in a National Hunt stable. He therefore took up full-time employment with Horace Smith as assistant to his father. During the winter Dick hunted, sometimes as often as five days a week, and either schooled young horses or showed them to prospective purchasers; in the summer he rode show hunters in the ring.

Doug told me that in complete contrast to himself, Dick is a very organised and methodical person, similar to his maternal grandmother. On one occasion in 1934, when the family was living in the large bungalow beside the yard at Holyport near Maidenhead, Dick, as always, had neatly laid out his cub-hunting kit the night before, prepared for the dawn start. Doug, who had just acquired his first motorbike, had been to a party with a girlfriend. He came back very late, coasting his bike down the drive so as not to wake the rest of the household. In an attempt to reach the safety of their room unheard, he climbed in through the bedroom window. Unfortunately, as he did so, earth from his boots landed on Dick's neatly-pressed shirt and jodhpurs and, as Doug says, there was the most almighty fuss the next morning.

In 1938, aged eighteen, it looked as though Dick's hopes of leaving home to work for a National Hunt trainer were over. His parents set up their own livery and dealing establishment at Embrook House near Wokingham and his help was needed there to make the business a success. However, the well-known dealer, Oliver Dixon,

DICK ON EIRE AT EMBROOK, 1938

asked Dick to ride his point-to-pointers in the 1939 season. Dick was delighted to hunt them, when free, so they should get their certificates but sadly Oliver died early in the New Year and the horses were sold before Dick got the chance to race-ride in public.

In early September 1939 when war broke out, hunting was curtailed and the 1940 point-to-point season cancelled before Christmas. Due to the uncertainty of the future, Vincent's business quickly dwindled and the need for Dick to stay at home had now come to an end.

CHAPTER 3

Six Years in the Royal Air Force

DICK IN TEL AVIV

*I*n early 1940 Dick made up his mind to join the forces before he was called up. A number of friends were serving in the Royal Scots Greys who were stationed at Edinburgh and still horsed. Accordingly, armed with suitable letters from the adjutant stating that the regiment would like to have Mr R. S. Francis as one of them, he went to the local recruiting office with a view to signing up. Dick, however, was too young and was offered a job only as an assistant cook in the infantry, but he decided he would rather not join the army just to be a cook.

On impulse Dick decided he wanted to become a pilot. The local Royal Air Force recruiting officer was very much more helpful than his army counterpart and only too keen to accommodate Dick's wish to join the RAF. 'Sign here to be an airframe rigger and once you are in you can re-muster for flying duties.' Dick soon found that being re-allocated from an airframe rigger to be

DICK ON HIS HOTEL VERANDA IN TEL AVIV, 1942

DICK AND HIS FRIEND JOE RIDING CAMELS IN FRONT OF THE PYRAMIDS

a pilot was virtually an impossible task and the next three years proved how determined a character he could be. Dutifully he went off to train as an airframe rigger, based near Coningsby in Lincolnshire, and in late 1940 he was shipped out via the Cape to the Middle East. He spent the next two years following the ebb and flow of the retreating and then advancing British Army across the desert repairing aeroplanes, but each month, without fail, he put in a written request to transfer to flying duties.

In early 1943, much to his amazement, his

thirty-seventh request was granted. He arrived in Southern Rhodesia, via the Red Sea and the Cape, for pilot training. It did not take Dick long to discover that the next best thing to riding a good horse in the hunting field was flying, and it

DICK LOOKING SUPERB IN HIS ROYAL AIR FORCE UNIFORM; WITH HIS WINGS AND HIS CAMPAIGN MEDAL, THE AFRICA STAR. AS DICK SAYS, 'THIS MUST HAVE BEEN THE FELLOW MARY FELL IN LOVE WITH'

is an established fact that good horsemen make excellent pilots due to their light hands. After nine months' training he graduated as a fighter pilot, and was then commissioned with the rank of Pilot Officer and returned to England in the early summer of 1944, just in time for the Normandy invasion.

During his first few weeks back, Dick mainly flew fighters escorting bombers. As more fighter pilots had been trained than were found to be needed he was transferred from Spitfires to Wellington bombers and served on these for most of the remainder of the war in Europe. In the late winter of 1944, Dick was switched once again from Wellingtons, to train as a glider pilot. Gliders were used to ferry infantry over obstacles, such as the Rhine, to form bridgeheads. Members of Dick's course were not put into the field and he was soon back to Wellingtons.

As the war in Europe came to a close, Dick converted again, this time to be a pilot in Coastal Command. Initially his task was to see that surrendering German submarines and ships behaved themselves and later he helped to train navigators. For the last few weeks of his air force career, Dick flew Lancasters. Miraculously, with so much active duty, Dick survived the whole of the Second World War totally unscathed.

In October 1945, Dick's cousin Nesta Evans, who lived in Weston-super-Mare was to marry a Royal Air Force Officer from Scotland and Dick was asked to be his best man. 'The first person I saw when I walked in – she was standing by the stairs – was Mary Brenchley. Mary had been at school with Nesta and was then a schoolmistress. We fell in love straightaway.' George Owen, who was to be Dick's first guv'nor, said of the love match, 'His love for Mary must have been powerful as Dick lived and slept horses. One would have thought he would have married someone with the same passion.'

DICK, IN UNIFORM, IS BEST MAN AT HIS COUSIN NESTA'S WEDDING;
THIS IS THE DAY HE MET MARY. FROM THE LEFT ARE DICK, SAM, NESTA
AND HER SISTER NANCY

CHAPTER 4

The First Winners – and a Wife

THE YEARS 1946–48

Soon after Nesta's wedding Dick was demobbed, and now the war was over he was needed at home to help run the family business at Embrook House. As soon as he was back working again with horses, his ambition to become a jockey re-emerged more strongly than ever. Luckily for Dick, his brother Doug had married Julia Thelwall by then and was working in Cheshire as Master of the Horse to Victor Dyke Dennis. Victor always had a few point-to-pointers and hunter chasers as also had Julia's father, Bob Thelwall.

During the winter of 1945/46 Dick was a regular visitor to hunt in Cheshire and as a result managed to get his first three rides. These are worth recording in full:

1. 23 March 1946
   Wynstay Point-to-Point
   Combined Members and Farmers Race
   Red Poker
   3rd in Members, won the Farmers Division

2. 13 April 1946
   Cheshire Farmers Bona Fide Meeting
   Hunt Maiden Chase
   Louis the Great
   Fell

3. 27 April 1946
   Bangor-on-Dee
   Hunter Chase
   Louis the Great
   Unplaced

Dick's first ride was in a standard point-to-point and then he rode in the Cheshire Farmers Bona Fide meeting. These meetings were very popular in the 1920s and 1930s and could best be described as halfway between point-to-pointing and proper National Hunt racing. Bangor-on-Dee, which was to prove a lucky course for Dick, was the venue for his third ride.

Life at Embrook House took up where it had left off after the rude interruption of the war with only a few changes. Mary Brenchley was a frequent visitor, coming to see Dick every second or third weekend, and he found that attending the horse shows no longer held the same appeal. Again he took up the quest for employment in a National Hunt stable, but with no more luck than he had had in the thirties when he had been turned down for being too small. This time there were no vacancies due to the severe curtailment of National Hunt racing which had stopped for the duration of the war. He had one advantage, however: he could at that time ride at 9st 10lb, the ideal weight for a tyro attempting to break into the ranks of National Hunt riders.

Salvation arrived in the early autumn of 1946 when Doug Francis arranged for Dick to go as secretary-cum-pupil trainer to George Owen who had recently taken out a public licence to train at Decoy Farm, near Chester. George came from a hunting family and had been a top jockey, first of all as an amateur, then as a professional. George's three biggest wins were the Cheltenham

Foxhunters on Melleray's Belle in 1930, the Cheltenham Gold Cup on Brendan's Cottage in 1939, and the Champion Chase at Liverpool on The Professor also in 1939.

Dick lived with the Owen family and was immediately accepted into Cheshire's sporting society. Although he lived there for only four years, Dick feels it is like returning home when he visits Cheshire each year when he comes over from America for the Grand National meeting: he is a trustee of Aintree Racecourse. In retrospect, the choice of George Owen as a start to his racing career was extraordinarily lucky, for in a period of only ten years, George started off three amateurs — Dick Francis, Tim Brookshaw and Stan Mellor, all of whom later became Champion NH Jockeys.

Dick's daily routine was simple. In the morning he rode out two or three lots which often involved schooling young horses, and in the afternoons he worked on George's accounts. It is worth remembering that when Dick arrived at Decoy Farm, he was nearly twenty-seven years old, a war veteran and an extremely experienced all-round horseman. Yet he had ridden only three times in public.

Within a few days of his arrival, George gave Dick his first ride in a race open to professionals at Woore, where he came fourth on Russian Hero. Obviously George was impressed with his pupil for he continued to give him rides. However, it must have been frustrating for Dick as he was sometimes jocked off a horse for a more fashionable rider even after it had run promisingly for him on a previous occasion.

Later that autumn George moved his stables to Cholmondeley Castle. The winter of 1946/47 was particularly severe and heavy snow fell throughout the British Isles; racing was stopped in England on 23 January and did not start again until 15 March. Even the National Hunt Festival was postponed for a week because of the inclement weather. Those eight weeks under snow were a grim time for everyone involved in racing, particularly so for National Hunt trainers who, at that time, did not of course have all-weather gallops, covered rides or indoor schools. It meant hours in the freezing cold for Dick and the other lads who worked the horses in circles on straw rings. March and April proved equally frustrating for although Dick was getting quite a few rides and being placed, he was unable to land a winner.

By the end of April, Dick must have been having doubts as to whether he would make the grade as a National Hunt jockey. However, on 2 May at Bangor-on-Dee his luck changed when Wrenbury Tiger carried him to a distance win in a hunter chase. Rompworthy came second in a handicap chase with Dick riding at 9st 13lb, and he finished off this memorable day with a double on Blitz Boy. Both winners were trained by George Owen, and before the end of the season

ROMPWORTHY AND DICK GOING TO POST AT LUDLOW. DICK RODE THIS HORSE 54 TIMES OUT OF HIS 101 RACES, WINNING 12

Dick had another seven winners, including three on Rompworthy who obliged for him on the Saturday and Monday of Cartmel.

Dick and Mary were now engaged and a date had been set for their wedding. On the last day of the season, Saturday 14 June, Dick went down to race at Newport, but lady luck had run out since Rompworthy was second, beaten a short head, and in the penultimate race of the entire season Wrenbury Sahib fell in a novice hurdle and Dick broke his collar-bone. The consequence of this was that he arrived at Paddington Chapel in London for his wedding on 21 June 1947 with his arm in a sling. Dick and Mary toured round Scotland for their honeymoon, Mary having to do all the driving while Dick read the maps.

After their honeymoon, Dick and Mary rented rooms at Faddiley near Nantwich for a few weeks. However, the young couple naturally wanted a home of their own, and were delighted when the Rae family, who lived at Higginsfield near Cholmondeley Castle, let them have a flat over the stables. Dick and Mary spent many happy hours here, refurbishing and decorating. Dick says of the Rae family: 'They were wonderful to us. Later Jane married John Boddington of the brewing family and Mary became God-mother to their son.'

Dick had a ride in the first race of the 1947/48 season at Newton Abbot but it was an inauspicious start when Hydora slipped up. He

Above: DICK AND DOUG WAIT OUTSIDE THE CHURCH ON DICK'S WEDDING DAY

Below: MARY AND HER SISTER JEAN RIDING AT BRACKLESHAM

Opposite: DICK AND MARY LEAVING THE CHURCH AFTER THEIR WEDDING

GEORGE OWEN'S TRAINING STRING IN THE GROUNDS OF
CHOLMONDLEY CASTLE

Opposite: IN THE WINNER'S ENCLOSURE AT BANGOR-ON-DEE.
DICK WON ON LIGHTHEAD, THE LAD IS FRANK PERKS AND THE
OWNER CHARLIE READ

had to wait until 30 August for his first winner, when Sandon walked over in a selling hurdle at Buckfastleigh. The season proceeded well – Rompworthy won a couple of races before Christmas and Dick also rode two winners on Russian Hero, one at Haydock and the other at Leicester. This was a good start for this obviously gifted amateur jockey.

In December, George Owen went to the Newmarket Sales and Dick was left in charge of the yard. He went round to give the horses their last feed at ten o'clock in the evening – something George always did himself when he was at home – and noticed that Russian Hero appeared to be suffering from colic, an extremely painful and sometimes fatal internal twisting of a horse's lower bowel. Dick immediately summoned the vet, Bobby O'Neil from Malpas, and with the help of the horse's lad they managed to get Russian Hero to his feet. Then on the instructions of the vet they walked him round the large enclosed yard until six o'clock the next morning, by which time the horse had recovered. There is a postscript to this episode which follows later.

By early March 1948, when the major meetings started, Dick had had well over 100 rides which was more than any other amateur, and only a few of the leading professionals exceeded this number. With ten winners notched up, he had several excellent rides booked for the Cheltenham Festival, Sandown's Grand Military meeting and the Grand National meeting at Aintree but when Dick arrived at Cheltenham he was asked to go and see the Stewards. They told him that he must either turn professional after

DICK UP ON RUSSIAN HERO, WINNING IN THE COUNTY CHASE AT HAYDOCK, NOVEMBER 1947

the Festival or limit his rides to amateur races only. Despite Dick's pleas to be allowed to remain an amateur for the rest of the season, the Stewards were adamant so he opted to become a professional at the end of the Festival meeting.

Ironically, that Cheltenham meeting did not go well for Dick. On the first day he was third in the now defunct United Hunts Challenge Cup on the strongly fancied Merry Knight. The second day saw him being unplaced in the 4-mile National Hunt Chase (the amateurs' Grand National) on Sam Spider and then he broke his collar-bone again when Russian Hero fell in the Seven Springs Handicap Chase: this meant he missed all of his rides on the third day, including those in the Kim Muir and the Foxhunters.

Sadly for Dick, he was merely a spectator at that year's Grand National meeting as he was still unfit to ride and it was not until 14 April that he had his first winner as a professional when Resurgent won a Novices Chase at Ludlow. His best day that season after turning professional was at Cartmel when from four rides he ended up with two winners and two seconds; the first winner was the aptly named Coastal Command, trained by his brother Doug who had by then taken out a trainer's licence. The season ended with Dick having sixteen winners, ten as an amateur and six as a professional.

DICK AND SAM SPIDER, NUMBER 47,
IN THE CHELTENHAM NATIONAL HUNT
STEEPLECHASE, MARCH 1948

DICK'S SECOND WIN AS A PROFESSIONAL; DOG WATCH JUMPING THE
LAST TO WIN A HANDICAP CHASE AT SOUTHWELL, APRIL 1948

CHAPTER 5

Lord Bicester and his Horses

THE 1948/49 AND 1949/50 SEASONS

GEORGE BEEBY'S STRING ON THE WAY TO EXERCISE ON THE BERKSHIRE
DOWNS. SILVER FAME LEADS ROIMOND

Since 1918, there have been five really out-standing owners in the National Hunt game – Her Majesty Queen Elizabeth The Queen Mother, for whom Dick rode some of his best races; Anne, Duchess of Westminster, a personal friend of Dick's, who owned the immortal Arkle and a succession of other top-class horses; Miss Dorothy Paget, for whom Dick rode a few times when her usual jockey Dave Dick was laid up; Mr Jimmy (J. V.) Rank, whose best horse, Prince Regent, was trained as was Arkle by the late Tom Dreaper, and last but not least, the highly successful merchant banker, the first Lord Bicester (Mr Vivian Hugh Smith prior to his elevation to the peerage).

By the autumn of 1948, Lord Bicester had the strongest team of steeplechasers in the country which was mainly trained by George Beeby at Compton in Berkshire; the string included Roimond, Finnure and Silver Fame, and arguably these, including Frank Vickerman's Cottage Rake, were the four best chasers then in training in England and Ireland. All of Lord Bicester's horses were great individuals, possibly because he was nearly always advised on their purchase by the top showman, Harry Bonner, and many of them were produced as young horses by Tom Dreaper. Harry was a great friend of Dick's father, and both families spent much time together. In fact, Dick had been briefly engaged to Harry's daughter, Beryl, before the war but the romance fizzled out when Dick joined the RAF and was posted to the Middle East. Harry had seen Dick's progress first as an amateur then a professional and it was he who advised Lord Bicester to invite Dick to be his second jockey. Martin Molony, Lord Bicester's first jockey, had a long-standing retainer in Ireland and went back to ride there each Saturday. Dick discussed this offer both with his brother Doug and also with George Owen, and finally decided to accept as he would be riding some of the finest horses in England, even if it were only on Saturdays.

At this point Dick had four ambitions in his life. One, to be Champion Jockey; two, to win the Grand National; three, to visit the United States and, four, to build his own house. This new opportunity to race the top-class horses should, he thought, help open the door to his racing quests.

There is no doubt that Dick was extremely fond of Lord Bicester. Indeed, one of Dick's most endearing traits is his unswerving loyalty to the trainers for whom he rode and their main owners. Lord Bicester obviously really loved his horses and summered them out to grass at his home, Tusmore Park near Bicester. Sadly the house was demolished on his death and the contents all sold. The wonderful racing photographic collection was lost as a result, and although the family have done their utmost to help supply some for this book, they have very few left. At least once a day Lord Bicester would visit his horses, always with some sugar lumps or nuts in his pocket with which to feed them. Dick recalls that 'One of the nicest things about the "old man" was going over to see him in the summer and walking out into the paddocks to enjoy watching the horses. He never said much. He just loved being with them.'

At the beginning of the season Dick continued to ride mainly for George Owen and his own brother Doug since George Beeby did not run Lord Bicester's horses until the ground became soft enough in late October or early November. In fact, the 1948/49 season started slowly with no winners until the last day of September when Dick rode the George Owen-trained Resurgent at Ludlow. His second win quickly followed at Hexham on 4 October on Lord Shrewsbury's Sam Spider.

Dick's first appearance in the famous Bicester colours of black with gold sleeves and red cap came at Nottingham on 26 October, when Parthenon was unplaced. A few days later Dick got his introduction to the unique Aintree fences when he was second, again on Parthenon, in the

Opposite: DICK ON ROIMOND. THEY WON A NUMBER OF RACES, BUT ARE BEST REMEMBERED FOR BEING SECOND IN THE 1949 GRAND NATIONAL

A PRESENTATION PHOTOGRAPH FROM THE EARL OF SHREWSBURY,
SHOWING SAM SPIDER WINNING AT HUNTINGDON IN OCTOBER 1948

Opposite: DICK ON FINNURE, PROBABLY HIS FAVOURITE HORSE. THEY WON
TWO GREAT RACES, THE KING GEORGE VI CHASE AT KEMPTON IN 1949 AND
THE 1950 CHAMPION CHASE AT THE LIVERPOOL GRAND NATIONAL MEETING

Grand Sefton Chase, the winner being Lecale Prince ridden by the Hon. Anthony Mildmay. Dick remembers that day well, '... especially jumping Becher's for the first time. Suddenly one could see for five miles across Liverpool.' On 30 October Dick won at Worcester on Roimond. On 13 November at Stratford-upon-Avon he won an Optional Seller on Silver Fame.

On 23 November, Dick had his first ride on Finnure – unsuccessful as they fell during the handicap chase at the now defunct Birmingham course. Dick regarded Finnure, a chestnut gelding, as the best horse he ever rode – including the two Gold Cup winners, Mont Tremblant and Silver Fame. Finnure was originally owned and trained by P. J. (Darkie) Prendergast who won the Irish Cesarewitch with him before winning with him under National Hunt Rules during the 1947/48 season. Like all Lord Bicester's horses, he was a superb looking individual, although he was slightly lighter than many of them and would have been a middleweight rather than a heavyweight hunter.

In the autumn of 1948, Finnure came over to England and like most of the other Bicester horses was trained by George Beeby. After the first unsuccessful outing, Dick won with him at Kempton on 4 December.

The King George VI Chase was and still is one of the most prestigious events in the racing calendar and the Boxing Day meeting at Kempton is acknowledged as the most important in December. In 1948, the first day's racing was frosted off so the second day's card was abandoned and the first day's card run on the second day instead. It was a highly successful meeting for Dick. He won the Chiswick Chase on Finnure and came second on Roimond to Cottage Rake in the King George VI.

In the space of only two years, Dick had gone from having no winners at all to brilliantly riding top-class horses. It is doubtful whether any other jockey has risen through the ranks quite so quickly.

The 1949 Grand National meeting was a four-day event, with the majority of the races run on the flat. Dick was greatly looking forward to it, having much enjoyed his introduction to the imposing fences the previous November with Parthenon. The first day, 23 March, started badly however when he fell at the second fence in the Topham Trophy. Matters did not improve on the second day when Silver Fame fell at the last in the Champion Chase with the race apparently won. Dick had no rides on the third day, for that was devoted mainly to flat racing.

Saturday 26 March was the day of the great race itself. Lord Bicester had two runners in the National – Roimond, the top weight, carrying 11st 12lb and Dick up on Parthenon, set to carry 10st. As usual, Martin Molony was in Ireland (this was only the second occasion on which the Grand National had been run on a Saturday – previously it had been held on Fridays), so Aubrey Brabazon, probably the most fashionable jockey on either side of the Irish Sea at the time, had been booked to ride Roimond. Unfortunately Aubrey had a nasty fall on Castledermot in the Stanley Chase on Thursday when leading the field at the Canal Turn. He had badly bruised his ankle and foot and was instructed to report to the racecourse doctor early on Saturday morning when he hoped to be passed fit to ride in the National.

Lord Bicester and his daughter, Dr Honor Vivian Smith, were there when the foot was inspected. The foot was badly damaged – not only was it bruised in all shades of black, purple and blue, but the toenails were bright red! The inspecting party took one look and Aubrey left the racecourse to catch the next flight back to Dublin. The previous night Aubrey had shared a

ROIMOND AT WORCESTER, OCTOBER 1948.
DICK'S FIRST WIN IN LORD BICESTER'S COLOURS

DICK ON FINNURE

DICK LEADS THE FIELD IN THE 1948 KING GEORGE VI CHASE ON
ROIMOND. THEY FINISHED SECOND TO THE MIGHTY COTTAGE RAKE
RIDDEN BY AUBREY BRABAZON

DICK LEADS DURING THE FIRST CIRCUIT IN THE STAYERS' HANDICAP CHASE
AT CHELTENHAM ON LORD BICESTER'S PARTHENON, DECEMBER 1948

room at the Adelphi Hotel with Dan Moore (another great Irish jockey who later trained the dual Gold Cup and Grand National winner L'Escargot). It transpired that for a joke Dan had painted the sleeping Aubrey's toenails with red nail varnish. This whole incident was perhaps unfortunate for Aubrey but certainly a godsend for Dick.

Roimond, despite being the top weight, was strongly fancied but was now without a jockey and, being the Grand National, all the leading jockeys were already booked. Lord Bicester, although disappointed at losing his main jockey, calmly told George Beeby, 'Dick can ride Roimond and you can find someone else for Parthenon.'

Every jockey who has ridden in the Grand National agrees that the hours leading up to the race are the most nerve-racking of their career. The atmosphere in the weighing-room can only be described as tense. Dr Honor told me that Dick was composed in the parade ring before he mounted Roimond and that she can remember being impressed by his equanimity – one of his great attributes as a jockey. As Dick and Roimond had top weight they led the parade, which must have been an ordeal in itself. When I was talking to Dick at the 1993 Grand National meeting, he said, 'You cannot imagine what it is like. All you can see is a huge sea of faces and you feel as if there are *millions* of people watching you.' Back then in the late forties, the race still attracted crowds in excess of 250,000 people; the course itself was much more formidable than it is today with fences that were virtually upright walls of timber dressed with spruce or gorse.

The tapes went up and Dick and Roimond jumped the first fence in the front wave, where Parthenon, with R. Bates up and carrying 5lb overweight, departed. They continued in the first six or so fences, across the Melling Road for the first time and led the field over the four fences in the home straight. All down the line of embankment fences to Becher's second time they were in front, Roimond jumping superbly. As they approached Becher's, Royal Mount took the lead and stayed there until the fence after Valentine's when he made an error. Ominously Roimond was now joined by Dick's old friend Russian Hero, ridden by Leo McMorrow. They raced neck and neck to the Melling Road when Russian Hero, with 18lbs less in the saddle, pulled away to win by a comfortable eight lengths. Royal Mount was a length behind in third place, having made a remarkable recovery, with the favourite, Cromwell ridden by Anthony Mildmay, in fourth place.

Ironically Russian Hero was the first horse which Dick had ridden against professionals. Dick knew the horse well and he was still trained by his old guv'nor, George Owen. As they had come back onto the racecourse for the second time Dick had thought Russian Hero might falter, as he was considered to be at his best over two and a half miles, but that day the horse found fresh reserves of stamina. He got his second wind and never came back at all.

Russian Hero's owner was Fernie Williamson, a tenant farmer on the Duke of Westminster's estate near Chester. Instead of retiring to the Adelphi Hotel, the traditional venue for the winners to celebrate with champagne, Fernie arranged a celebration dinner at The Blossoms Hotel in Chester. When Dick was called upon to say a few words about Leo McMorrow, the winning jockey, he said laughingly: 'I am delighted at your success, but if I had known Russian Hero was going to beat me that night when he had colic, I would have let the bugger die.' The party that night went down in Grand National folklore as a party to end all parties.

A few days after the National, George Beeby

THE PARTY TO CELEBRATE RUSSIAN HERO'S GRAND NATIONAL WIN, AT
THE BLOSSOMS HOTEL, CHESTER. FROM LEFT TO RIGHT: MRS WILLIAMSON,
LEO MCMORROW, MRS OWEN, GEORGE OWEN, FERNIE WILLIAMSON AND,
SEATED, DICK

GEORGE OWEN (ON THE EXTREME LEFT OF THE PICTURE) AND FRIENDS
OUTSIDE CHOLMONDLEY CASTLE THE MORNING AFTER RUSSIAN HERO
WON THE GRAND NATIONAL. DICK IS ON THE FAR RIGHT

asked Dick to school a horse called Hereford which was trained by Ken Cundell. The pair immediately clicked and Ken engaged Dick to ride him in a novice chase at Cheltenham the following week. They won easily and from then on Dick regularly rode for both Ken and his cousin Frank for whom he won an astonishing fifteen races from only twenty-two rides on Crudwell.

HEREFORD WINNING AT CHELTENHAM, APRIL 1949. DICK'S FIRST RIDE OF MANY FOR KEN CUNDELL

FIGHTING LINE GOING OUT TO WIN THE WELSH GRAND NATIONAL AT CHEPSTOW,
APRIL 1949

The season ended brilliantly for Dick which must have helped him overcome the disappointment of Aintree. On Easter Tuesday, Dick rode Fighting Line, trained by Ken Cundell, to an easy victory in the Welsh Grand National at Chepstow; this was the most important win of Dick's career to date. Another historic victory came later in the week at Bangor-on-Dee when he rode his first treble. Mass, also trained by Frank Cundell, won a novice hurdle; Rompworthy, now trained by Dick's brother Doug, won a 2-mile handicap and Tommy Thrush completed the treble with a win in a 2-mile novice chase.

Cartmel again proved successful with two wins from only four rides. All in all, Dick's first season as a professional was highly successful and he ended up with twenty-three winners.

Rompworthy and Dick were successful for the last time when Dick got his first win of the 1949/50 season on this small, untidy gelding at Worcester on 20 September. Dick's first ride on him had been on 2 November 1946 in a 3-mile chase at Worcester when they pulled up; it was only Dick's second ride in public after he had joined George Owen. The five winners Dick had on Rompworthy in 1947 were particularly important as they undoubtedly helped to get him noticed when he was still a 'claiming' amateur, and no doubt the riding fees in his first season as a professional did not go amiss. In all, Dick rode Rompworthy in fifty-four races, winning on twelve occasions and coming second or third on another eighteen.

As far as the quality of winners go, the 1949/50 season was probably Dick's greatest. He rode important winners at all the major meetings – the Kempton Boxing Day meeting, the National Hunt Festival and the Grand National meeting.

In late October Dick and Mary were temporarily apart: Dick had to go north from Cheshire to ride at Kelso and then planned to travel to Cheltenham to stay with an uncle before riding at Chepstow; Mary went to London to stay with her mother. During the week, Dick telephoned Mary a few times and she told him she was not feeling particularly well, but put the symptoms down to 'flu. Eventually she saw a doctor who diagnosed infantile paralysis – polio – and was immediately admitted to Neasden Isolation Hospital. It was a very worrying time for Dick who returned to the hospital most nights,

YEW TREE HOUSE, DICK AND MARY'S HOME IN COMPTON, A FEW YARDS DOWN
THE LANE FROM RODEN HOUSE

driving from racecourses all over the country.

While Mary was recovering in hospital, Ken Cundell made arrangements for them to move into Yew Tree House in Compton which was close to Roden House, where he trained. Dick and Mary moved in the following March just after the National Hunt Festival. Dick was quite sad about leaving his friends in Cheshire; however, it was very difficult living on one side of the country and riding in another. He had a new racing career in front of him riding Lord Bicester's top horses, but would still ride for George Owen and his brother Doug when he was available.

Dick's first big winner of the 1949/50 season came on Monday 26 December when he rode an inspired race to get Finnure home by three-quarters of a length from Cottage Rake in the King George VI Chase. Not surprisingly, as he had won the last two Gold Cups (and was soon to win a third), Cottage Rake was 4/6 on favourite. Ridden as usual by Aubrey Brabazon, 'The Brab', Cottage Rake led into the straight. Dick and Finnure joined them between the last two fences, but it was only after the last that they started to pull away. Sweet victory. It was one of the most thrilling finishes ever of this great race and indeed one of the greatest races of Dick's life.

Dr Honor says it also was her father's most thrilling day's racing, although he went on to win the Gold Cup with Silver Fame in 1951. Not only was the race extremely close but they nearly failed to reach the racecourse as their car broke down en route.

Dick was involved in another tight finish on the second day of the Cheltenham National Hunt Festival. Riding Tommy Thrush, he was engaged in a duel from two out with Bob Turnell on Dominic's Bar in the Seven Springs Chase. Dick went on to win by a length.

In the Champion Chase at Liverpool, Dick was once again reunited with Finnure. Since winning at Kempton, Finnure had been second under Martin Molony to Cottage Rake in the Gold Cup. Once again there was a desperate struggle between the two tough and strong jockeys riding hammer and tongs from two out. His opponents this time were Arthur Thompson and Coloured Schoolboy. Finnure held on by a length, having come under tremendous pressure in the last one hundred yards. Another great victory.

Dick had great hopes for the Grand National as he was to be reunited once more with Roimond who had been second the previous year and was joint favourite at 10–1 for the 1950 race. Roimond had two ways of running: either he tried hard and bowled along happily in the front, or he sulked in mid-division and did not try. By the time they had reached the first fence, Dick knew it was one of the 'not trying' days. Roimond muddled along, jumping indifferently and fell quite soon, at the fence after Becher's.

However, much more important than Liverpool that year was the birth of Dick's eldest son, Merrick, on 1 April. Dick was riding at Bangor-on-Dee that day where for once he did not have a winner. Dick gave fellow jockey Derek Ancil a lift south and says he terrified Derek by driving at heart-stopping speed all the way to the Radcliffe Hospital in Oxford. Merrick has obviously inherited the Francis family's horse-loving genes as he has become the fourth generation to ride winners under rules and now runs one of Europe's largest racehorse transport companies, which is based in Lambourn, Berkshire.

By the end of the season, Dick had increased his total winners to twenty-nine but it was the three important wins described in detail above and his second in the Grand National which stamped him as one of the leading jockeys in only his second full season as a professional.

ROIMOND AND DICK OUT IN FRONT TO WIN AT
KEMPTON. THE JOCKEY ON THE EXTREME LEFT IS
BRYAN MARSHALL

KNUCKLE DUSTER AND A. JARVIS JUMP THE LAST BEAUTIFULLY TO WIN THE
BECHER'S OPEN CHASE AT SANDOWN, MARCH 1950. THE HORSE DIVING
THROUGH THE FENCE IS THE FOLLY, RIDDEN BY DICK. THE FACT THAT THEY
DID NOT FALL IS A TRIBUTE TO DICK'S HORSEMANSHIP

DICK IS LED OUT ON FINNURE BEFORE WINNING THE CHAMPION CHASE AT
THE 1950 GRAND NATIONAL MEETING

ROIMOND (NUMBER 2) JUMPING BECHER'S BROOK IN THE 1950 GRAND
NATIONAL. THE HORSE ON THE FAR RIGHT IS FREEBOOTER, RIDDEN BY
JIMMY POWER, THE EVENTUAL WINNER

CHAPTER 6

Compton Based

THE 1950/51, 1951/52 AND 1952/53 SEASONS

The 1950/51 season was Dick's most successful to date and he rode thirty winners. Before Christmas, his best win was in the Molyneux Chase at Liverpool on the Duchess of Norfolk's Possible, trained by W. Payne, but undoubtedly the highlight of the year was at Kempton's Christmas meeting.

On the first day he won a 3-mile chase on Lord Bicester's Bluff King and he followed this up by riding the same owner's Silver Fame to be second in the King George VI Chase behind Her Majesty The Queen's (now HM Queen Elizabeth The Queen Mother) Manicou. He then won the Chiswick Chase over $2\frac{1}{2}$ miles, once more on Possible. Dick said to me, 'I loved those two rides on Possible at Liverpool and Kempton. Possible just slayed the opposition over the big jumps.'

On the second day at Kempton, Dick won the Christmas Handicap Hurdle on Coup d'Épée, trained by Ken Cundell. At that time, this was a very important race and was the biggest hurdle win of Dick's career.

Dick and Mary had great cause to celebrate in February the next year when their second son, Felix, was born.

In the 1951 Grand National, Dick rode Finnure and had high hopes of getting round successfully. The race got off to a very ragged start and sadly Finnure was brought down at the first – he did not fall as the form-books state. It was a race full of incidents with only two horses finishing the race without falling. Alas, Finnure damaged a hock in the fall which ended his racing career. He was given to Bruce Hobbs as a trainer's hack.

July 1951 was extremely wet so the season got under way with good rather than firm going in the West Country, resulting in more runners than usual for the time of year. Dick opened his account with Fighting Line on the second day of the season. The Liverpool November meeting must have been frustrating for Dick for he was beaten a short head on Possible in the Molyneux Chase and by half a length in the Becher's Chase on Irish Lizard; however, at Kempton's Boxing Day meeting he won the Oaklands Chase on Senlac Hill.

At the first day of the Cheltenham National Hunt Festival, Dick had a fall from Seravik II in the National Hunt Juvenile Chase which put him out of action for the rest of the meeting. This race was limited to horses which had just turned four (the same age as those which run in the Triumph Hurdle at today's Festival meeting), and most jockeys were only too pleased when it was scrapped.

In the 1952 Grand National Dick rode Skyreholm, one of the horses trained by Neville Crump, but they fell at the seventh; Crump wasn't too disappointed as he won the race with Teal.

DICK ON THE LEFT, UP ON THE FOLLY AT THE SECOND FENCE IN THE
HANDICAP CHASE AT CHELTENHAM, NOVEMBER 1950

Opposite: DICK ON THE DUCHESS OF NORFOLK'S BIG CHASER, POSSIBLE.
DICK WON SOME GOOD RACES ON HIM, INCLUDING THE MOLYNEUX
CHASE AT LIVERPOOL, NOVEMBER 1950

DICK ON COUP D'ÉPÉE BEFORE WINNING THE 1950 CHRISTMAS HURDLE
AT THE KEMPTON BOXING DAY MEETING. THIS WAS HIS THIRD AND
ALSO HIS BIGGEST WIN OF THE MEETING

DICK AND FINNURE LEADING FIRST TIME ROUND IN THE STANLEY
STEEPLECHASE AT SANDOWN PARK, JANUARY 1951

DICK AND ROIMOND IN THE GRAND NATIONAL HANDICAP CHASE,
SANDOWN, JANUARY 1951. NEAREST TO THE CAMERA IS THE EVENTUAL
WINNER ARCTIC GOLD, WITH T. MOLONEY UP

COUP D'ÉPÉE AND DICK IN QUILTED COLOURS AND NOSEBAND FLYING
OVER THE FIRST FENCE IN THE HAMPTON NOVICE CHASE, KEMPTON,
JANUARY 1951

DICK AND ROMAN FIRE BEING LED TO THE START OF THE WELSH GRAND
NATIONAL, EASTER 1951. THEY WERE UNPLACED

Opposite: COUP D'ÉPÉE – HIS GIRTH HAS SLIPPED BACK DUE TO A HUGE
LEAP EARLIER IN THE RACE

THE START OF THE 1951 WELSH GRAND NATIONAL. ROMAN FIRE AND DICK ARE IN THE CENTRE OF THE PICTURE AT THE BACK

THE FALLERS AT THE FIRST FENCE, GRAND
NATIONAL, 1951. FROM LEFT TO RIGHT:
PADDY FITZGERALD, BRYAN MARSHALL,
DICK FRANCIS, PAT TAAFFE, BOB
MCCREERY, JACK DOWDESWELL AND
MICHAEL SCUDAMORE. MICK O'DWYER IS
BENDING DOWN

FIVE HORSES IN FRONT OF RODEN HOUSE. DICK IS IN THE CENTRE ON
SUN FLAME AND FRANK CHAPMAN IS ON THE FAR LEFT

Opposite: DICK ON THE FRENCH-BRED MARE TCHESKA, PATRICIA ELLERY
LEADING

IRISH LIZARD AND DICK JUMPING THE CHAIR BEFORE FINISHING
SECOND IN THE BECHERS CHASE AT AINTREE, NOVEMBER 1951

SILVER FAME AND DICK AT SANDOWN IN THE HANLEY CHASE, JANUARY 1952

THE OPEN DITCH IN FRONT OF THE STANDS AT SANDOWN IN THE EWELL
CHASE, DECEMBER 1952. MICHAEL SCUDAMORE ON ESB LEADS CAPTAIN
W. GIBSON ON GREENOGUE, WITH DICK ON THE WINNER, MONT TREMBLANT

All in all, the 1951/52 season was a slightly disappointing one for Dick – only twenty-eight winners in total compared to thirty the previous season and the only really important win was the Christmas Hurdle.

1952/53 proved to be very much better than the previous season in every way and Dick ended up with thirty-eight winners, the third best total of his riding career.

Undoubtedly, the best horse Dick rode that season was Mont Tremblant, owned by Dorothy Paget and trained by Fulke Walwyn; the combination had won the previous season's Gold Cup, with stable jockey Dave Dick. However, Dave Dick broke his leg in mid-season and Dick was asked to stand in for him. Dick and Mont Tremblant had a brilliant record for they won the Ewell Chase at Sandown on 11 December, were second in the King George VI Chase on Boxing Day to Halloween and then won the Stanley Chase at Sandown on 16 January.

Shortly after Dick's December win on Mont Tremblant at Sandown, he had his first public

MONT TREMBLANT LANDING OVER THE LAST FENCE AND FIRST PAST THE
POST IN THE BIG KEMPTON RACE, DECEMBER 1952

ride on Crudwell when they won the prestigious Henry VIII Chase at Hurst Park over 3 miles. Crudwell was one of the greatest and most popular horses of the 1950s; he was owned by Mrs Bunny Cooper and was named after the Wiltshire village where he was foaled. Apart from his numerous successes under National Hunt Rules, he was also a useful horse on the flat when younger, winning all distances from ten to sixteen furlongs. He was second in the 1952 Ascot Stakes at the Royal meeting when ridden by Lester Piggott.

After their first win at Sandown, Dick realised that he had met a star in the making. Over the next few seasons, Dick had many successes on Crudwell although, due to his prior commitments to other trainers, he could not ride him on every occasion.

The National Hunt Festival saw Dick being second in the Cathcart Chase on Wigby and third in the National Hunt Handicap Chase on Domata. He rode the Peter Cazalet-trained Statecraft in the Gold Cup, which was to be the first of many rides for the stable. Irish

Lizard made amends for being beaten in the Becher's Chase the previous season when he and Dick won a very hotly contested Topham Trophy at the 1953 Grand National meeting. Irish Lizard was owned by Lord Sefton who had recently sold Aintree Racecourse to Mirabel Topham.

In the National, Dick opted to ride what he called 'a real bonecrusher' in Lord Bicester's Senlac Hill. Most experienced jockeys would have politely declined to ride him round even a park course and would not have entertained the idea of riding 'that brainless animal' in a race such as the Grand National. Dick had already ridden Senlac Hill six times that season; they had completed the course three times and on the other three occasions Senlac Hill had fallen, normally into the open ditch. However Dick's gamble – be it bravery or not – paid off. In atrocious conditions – to quote Lord Bicester's daughter, Dr Honor, 'The ground would have bogged down a duck' – they completed the course, albeit coming in last of the five finishers from thirty-one starters.

DICK IS LED OUT ON CRUDWELL AT HURST PARK, FEBRUARY 1953. THEY FINISHED THIRD IN THE NEW CENTURY CHASE

DICK AND CRUDWELL IN THE WELSH GRAND NATIONAL
AT CHEPSTOW, APRIL 1955. THEY FINISHED TENTH

DICK ON MR HUGH SUMNER'S WIGBY AT NEWBURY. THEY WON THE
HUNGERFORD HANDICAP CHASE IN JANUARY 1953

CHELTENHAM GOLD CUP, 1953. TEAL LEADS AT THE FIRST. DICK IS ON
STATECRAFT, NUMBER 15, THIRD FROM THE REAR

DICK IS LED OUT ON IRISH LIZARD BEFORE WINNING THE
TOPHAM TROPHY AT THE 1953 GRAND NATIONAL MEETING.
REMARKABLY, IRISH LIZARD ALSO RAN IN THE GRAND
NATIONAL TWO DAYS LATER

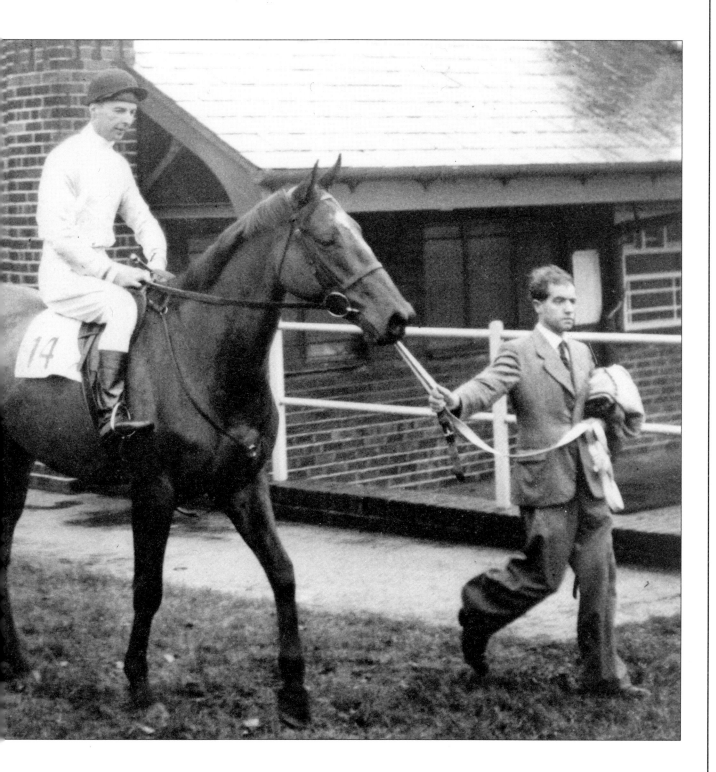

Soon afterwards Dick was appointed first jockey to Peter Cazalet who was based at Fairlawne near Tonbridge in Kent. He had one of the strongest teams of National Hunt horses in the country at the time and amongst his owners were the Queen and HM Queen Elizabeth, the Queen Mother.

Peter Cazalet was a trainer of the old school. Before the war he had been a useful amateur rider and while serving in the Welsh Guards with Anthony Mildmay during the war, the pair laid plans to turn his lovely estate, Fairlawne, into a major National Hunt yard. For nearly thirty years, until his much mourned premature death in 1973, it was highly successful. Peter Cazalet attracted rich sportsmen who purchased the best raw material. He oversaw the horses' work and schooling, while the yard was run by his legendary head lad, the Scotsman Jim Fairgrieve. The yard itself was immaculate with not a straw out of place and cobwebs did not dare to appear. Likewise, the lads and the horses were always impeccably turned out.

Peter's son, His Honour Sir Edward Cazalet, QC, who is now a High Court Judge, remembers Dick's association with his father with great fondness. When I went to interview Sir Edward, who hadn't seen Dick for some ten years, he talked of him as if he were an elder brother. He told me that Dick was a great thinker and although in his day when jockeys were schooling horses they would just turn their caps back to front and ride with no protection, Dick always wore a skull cap. Nowadays, of course, it is compulsory under Jockey Club Rules for anyone riding a racehorse to wear proper head protection, whether they are riding out or schooling.

SENLAC HILL WINNING THE FELCOURT HANDICAP CHASE AT LINGFIELD

MONAVEEN LEADING THE STRING AT FAIRLAWNE, PETER CAZALET
SUPERVISES

Opposite: PETER CAZALET (LEFT) WITH JIM FAIRGRIEVE (CENTRE) AND
ARTHUR FREEMAN (RIGHT) AT FAIRLAWNE

KEMPTON PARK, 1959. EDWARD CAZALET (ON THE LEFT) JUMPING THE
LAST ON LOCHROE TO WIN FROM SERINGAPATAM (BILL REES)

Opposite: MARAIS HALL, OWNED AND TRAINED BY KEN CUNDELL. DICK
RODE THIS HORSE ONCE IN THE CURFEW NOVICE CHASE AT WINDSOR IN
FEBRUARY 1952

CHAPTER 7

The Championship Season

1953/54

The 1953/54 season, with Dick riding as first jockey to Peter Cazalet, started in fine style. By 12 August, after only four days' racing, Dick had ridden five winners for his new guv'nor. From then on, the winners flowed in, mainly in novice hurdles and chases. Ken Cundell considers that one of Dick's great strengths as a jockey was the good ride he always gave horses, invariably getting them to the last with the minimum of fuss and effort. Dick loved race riding, and it can truly be said of him that he was paid to do what he liked doing best and clearly horses enjoyed racing when he rode them, indeed he had the kindest hands in the business: some described his having hands of silk. Examples of this would be Lochroe, owned by the late Lord Mildmay's sister, Mrs J. Mildmay-White, who won three novice hurdles on the trot by mid-November as did Three Gates with three novice chases in the same period.

Dick rode M'as-tu-vu for the first time on 26 October at Nottingham where they were second. Subsequently, he piloted HM Queen Elizabeth The Queen Mother's horse to three consecutive wins. The first was the Whitelaw Challenge Cup at Fontwell on 5 November, the second the Wimbledon Handicap at Kempton on 27 November, and the third, and most important, the Blindley Heath Handicap Chase at Lingfield on 5 December.

In November Dick had a purple patch. At the two-day meeting at Sandown on 21 and 22 November, he had six mounts – and produced three winners, two seconds and a third. Unusually, Dick did not have a winner at Kempton's Boxing Day meeting, but was third in the King George VI Chase on Mariner's Log. However, he did have a very nice win at Cheltenham's New Year meeting on Lord Abergavenny's Legal Prince.

Dick and Mary, happy as they were at Yew Tree House, wanted to build their own home and they found a site nearby at Blewbury; in December 1953, work started on their bungalow, Penny Chase, and they moved in in August 1954. Thus was one of Dick's ambitions fulfilled.

Later, on 15 January, he had a treble at Sandown when his first winner, Deal Park, got the better of Lester Piggott on Stranger. It is strange to think that these two great jockeys – top of their professions in National Hunt and Flat racing – actually raced against each other. The families became close friends and when Lester first retired (prior to his successful comeback in 1990), it was to Dick he turned to write his official biography which was published in 1986.

Opposite: DICK GOES OUT AT KEMPTON ON MRS J. MILDMAY-WHITE'S LOCHROE. THIS IS SIR EDWARD CAZALET'S FAVOURITE PHOTOGRAPH OF DICK

IN THE UNSADDLING ENCLOSURE AFTER M'AS-TU-VU HAS WON THE
BLINDLEY HEATH HANDICAP CHASE AT LINGFIELD, DECEMBER 1953.
HM QUEEN ELIZABETH THE QUEEN MOTHER AND HRH PRINCESS
MARGARET ENTER THE WINNER'S ENCLOSURE

Opposite: M'AS-TU-VU, THE WINNER, JUMPS THE LAST FENCE IN THE
WIMBLEDON HANDICAP CHASE, KEMPTON, NOVEMBER 1953

GOING, GOING . . .

GONE. MAILED FIRST, OWNED BY THE MARQUESS OF ABERGAVENNY,
GOES DOWN AT THE LAST IN THE KEMPTON HANDICAP, DECEMBER 1953

PENNY CHASE IN WINTER. MARY WAS AT THE CONTROLS OF THE LIGHT
AIRCRAFT FROM WHICH THIS PHOTOGRAPH WAS TAKEN

Above right: DICK'S SONS WITH THEIR GRANDMOTHER, JANET BRENCHLEY,
AT PENNY CHASE. MERRICK IS ON THE LEFT ON HIS FIRST PONY,
JOAN OF ARC, FELIX IS ON SMOKY

Below right: DICK AT THE WHEEL OF HIS MUCH-PRIZED JAGUAR, WITH
MERRICK AND FELIX IN THE BACK

CRUDWELL BEING LED IN AFTER WINNING THE NATIONAL TRIAL
HANDICAP CHASE AT LEICESTER, FEBRUARY 1954

The National Hunt Festival came and went without any winners. In the 1954 Grand National Dick rode Icy Calm who was having his first run of the season. He went well until The Chair when the horse tired, slowed down and started to jump badly. Dick pulled him up after three miles.

After the Grand National meeting, Dick had a double at Bangor-on-Dee on 3 April with Pondapatarri and Trambeza. The latter was Dick's seventy-eighth and last winner of the season. On 10 April, he rode Pondapatarri in a novice chase at the Beaufort Hunt meeting in Gloucestershire. Pondapatarri fell, bringing down Knight Sky. The

DICK RISES TO MAKE HIS SPEECH ON WINNING THE 1953/54 JOCKEY
CHAMPIONSHIP WITH SEVENTY-SIX WINNERS

latter landed right on top of Dick, crushing three vertebrae. It was only due to the skill of the great surgeon and physiotherapist, Bill Tucker, that Dick was able to ride again that season. Mr Tucker put Dick in plaster for two days and made him a leather brace with steel plates in the back, which Dick could remove when necessary.

Amazingly, Dick was fit enough to travel by sea in May to the United States of America to ride Rose Park, trained by Peter Cazalet and owned by Dick Wilkins, in an international chase at Belmont Park. In those days air travel for horses was in its infancy and none of the British contingent ran well. However, another of Dick's

ambitions had been fulfilled for not only did he want to visit and travel in America to expand his horizons, he had now raced there as well.

The only other time Dick rode abroad was at the famous Galway Festival in August 1951. He had gone over to ride Southern Coup in the main race, the Galway Plate, a handicap chase over 2 ½ miles. The course was, at that time, mainly un-railed, which was disconcerting for English jockeys who were not used to riding flat out into crowds who only stepped back as the horses approached. The trainer of Dick's mount in the big race was so worried about this that he got him a ride on Furthermore in the Salthill Handicap Hurdle to give him a little experience of riding under Irish conditions. Both horses were owned by Capt. E. A. Gargan and, although unplaced in the main race, Dick picked up a second in the hurdle.

Although Dick finished his British season in mid-April, he was an easy winner of the Jockey's Championship with seventy-eight winners. The runner-up, R. Emery, had fifty-eight. Dick had ridden in 331 races that season, more than any other jockey. Bryan Marshall, the previous Champion, had 288 rides, so Dick had worked really hard from early August right through to mid-April. By modern standards, it may not seem a lot to land a Champion Jockeyship with seventy-eight winners. However, in the early fifties, it was

THE DINNER PARTY AT THE CAFÉ DE PARIS TO CELEBRATE CRUDWELL'S THIRTIETH WIN, 12 JANUARY 1957. FROM LEFT TO RIGHT: GEOFFREY FRITH, CLERK OF THE COURSE AT MANCHESTER, SUSAN INGALL, AN ARTIST WHO PAINTED CRUDWELL, CHARLES COOPER, INEZ GREY, DICK, BARBARA CUNDELL, SIR FRANCIS WALSHE, MOLLY COOPER, FRANK CUNDELL, AND MARY

DICK, SECOND FROM THE LEFT, WITH CATH AND FULKE WALWYN AT THE
CENTRE OF THE HORSESHOE, ATTENDING A CELEBRATORY LUNCH
IN LONDON

a highly satisfactory total. Dick was naturally thrilled to be Champion Jockey, and considered it a great honour. It was a particularly good season for him, as not only was he Champion Jockey but he also had the privilege of riding winners in the Royal colours for the first time. Dick had fulfilled one more of his ambitions. One more to go.

National Hunt racing in those days was completely different from the sport which we now know. There were far fewer meetings, no evening meetings, and no question of helicopters, so there was no question of a jockey being able to ride at more than one racecourse in a day.

CHAPTER 8

Mainly Royal Rides

THE 1954/55, 1955/56 AND 1956/57 SEASONS

Dick's first winner of the 1954/55 season came with Diego Rubio on 14 August at Newton Abbot. Edward Cazalet, Peter Cazalet's son, had gone down with Dick to the West Country and the pair was sharing the stable's rides. The first few months of the season went reasonably well with Lochroe winning his first three novice chases off the reel, the last being the important Henry VIII Chase at Hurst Park on 18 December.

At the Kempton Boxing Day meeting Dick won the Chiswick Chase for Lord Bicester again, this time on Cintra. He was beaten a head by Fred Winter on Syrtre in the Christmas Handicap Hurdle and he was again third in the King George VI Chase on Mariner's Log.

Due to a heavy snowstorm the 1955 Cheltenham Festival meeting was reduced to two days, showing the sense of later years of moving on the date by a week. Dick had four rides at the Festival, but he did not ride into a place. In the Grand National, he rode Lord Bicester's Mariner's Log again but they fell at the first. His best win, near the end of the season, was at the Royal Artillery Meeting at Sandown where Crudwell won a decent Stayers Chase. Dick had another hard-working season with 283 rides yielding thirty-three winners but this was not a particularly satisfactory strike rate for him.

The 1955/56 season, Dick's third as stable jockey to Peter Cazalet, brought high expectations of a repeat of the successes of the 1953/54 season. He started well with Legal Prince, by now owned by Peter Cazalet, winning on the second day at Newton Abbot. He had another winner on the third day of the season.

The real highlight of the season prior to Christmas were the performances of Her Majesty Queen Elizabeth The Queen Mother's Devon Loch. Dick and Devon Loch started off with a warm-up in a novice hurdle at Sandown in mid-November when they finished a very respectable fourth. Their next outing was in the Blindley Heath Chase at Lingfield on 25 November, the first time Devon Loch had attempted a 3-mile race. He stayed the trip well and sprinted away from a useful field after the last. When interviewed after the race by the *Sporting Life*, Dick said of Devon Loch, 'He strikes me as being much more of a Liverpool horse than a Gold Cup one,' and he later said to Peter Cazalet, 'This is a real Aintree horse. I'd love to ride him there.'

Dick and Devon Loch appeared again together on 14 December in the Sandown Chase. Dick took the lead going down the back straight for the last time with Cottage Lace and Mariner's Log in close attendance. From the Pond fence onwards, Dick had Devon Loch flat out. He was lucky to win by three-quarters of a length, as Cottage Lace met the last wrong and lost four or five lengths when closing. It was clear from this run that Devon Loch had unlimited stamina and he became a very live candidate indeed for the Grand National.

DEVON LOCH GOING OUT FOR THE BLINDLEY HEATH STEEPLECHASE AT
LINGFIELD, NOVEMBER 1955

Opposite: DEVON LOCH CLEARING THE WATER JUMP IN THE BLINDLEY
HEATH STEEPLECHASE

M'AS-TU-VU CLEARING THE WATER JUMP IN THE ERIDGE
CHASE AT LINGFIELD, NOVEMBER 1955

SANDOWN HANDICAP CHASE, DECEMBER 1955. DOMATA (A. CORBETT), NUMBER 14, AND HM QUEEN ELIZABETH THE QUEEN MOTHER'S DEVON LOCH LEAD OVER THE OPEN DITCH

Opposite: THE KING GEORGE VI CHASE, 1955. DEVON LOCH RIDDEN BY BRYAN MARSHALL LEADS, WITH DICK ON LOCHROE GETTING TOO CLOSE TO THE FENCE BEFORE FALLING

At Kempton's Boxing Day meeting Dick had mixed luck. He won a novice chase on Hugh Sumner's Greek Flame, but fell in the King George VI Chase on Lochroe when he was strongly fancied to win. As first jockey for the stable and since Lochroe was the more fancied horse, Dick had opted for Lochroe while Bryan Marshall was unplaced on Devon Loch.

The big race for Dick at the National Hunt Festival was the National Hunt Handicap Chase when he was again teamed up with Devon Loch, his intended Grand National mount. In the paddock before the race, Peter Cazalet told Dick to 'give him a nice race' and Her Majesty Queen Elizabeth The Queen Mother added, 'Yes, but it would be nice to win this one on the way to Aintree.' Dick and Devon Loch finished a very respectable third carrying 11st 8lb, considerably more than the two horses which finished in front of them.

PETER CAZALET GIVES DICK A LEG UP ON
DEVON LOCH IN THE PADDOCK AT THE 1956
CHELTENHAM FESTIVAL, WATCHED BY THE
ROYAL PARTY. DICK FINISHED THIRD IN THE
NATIONAL HUNT HANDICAP CHASE, A
PROMISING PREPARATION RACE FOR THE
GRAND NATIONAL

Everything was now set for the 1956 Grand National where Devon Loch was set to carry 11st 4lb and was very well supported in the market at 100/7. The race is easy to describe. Armorial III took the lead at the first fence and until the water was followed by a group including the Queen Mother's M'as-tu-vu, ridden by Arthur Freeman, Sundew, Eagle Lodge, ESB, Ontray and Devon Loch. Sundew fell at Becher's second time round and Armorial III went at the fence after Valentine's, where Dick and Devon Loch took the lead. As they crossed the Melling Road, Dick was a couple of lengths clear of Eagle Lodge, ESB, Gentle Moya and Ontray. At the second last he was just ahead of Eagle Lodge, ESB and Ontray who then unseated his rider. Between the last two fences, ears pricked, Devon Loch started to show his superiority and landed clear over the last from ESB.

Dick and Devon Loch continued to gallop away from the toiling ESB throughout the long run-in and as they approached the post, he was obviously still full of running. Some fifty yards from the line, however, when Dick had the race in his pocket, Devon Loch suddenly staggered and more or less sat down – pancaked is the word most often used – with his front legs stretched in front of him and his back legs behind him – an equine spread-eagle. Devon Loch did not fall over and Dick somehow retained his seat. As the horse struggled to his feet, he was passed by ESB. It could still have been possible for him to be second, so Dick urged him forward, but he was all at sea and seemed to have temporarily lost control of his legs. Dick immediately dismounted.

No one will ever know what happened in those few seconds. Did Devon Loch see an imaginary jump? Did the horse have a minor heart attack, or was he startled for one crucial moment by the cacophony of cheers greeting the Royal winner?

Undoubtedly the cause of Devon Loch's collapse will remain one of racing's great unsolved mysteries. Dick himself believes it was the roar of the crowd which temporarily upset Devon Loch. Few men have ever come closer to winning a National and not done so. Dick nearly fulfilled his fourth and final ambition – but it was not to be.

It was a body-blow to all concerned, not only Her Majesty Queen Elizabeth The Queen Mother, but also Peter Cazalet who had been robbed before of training a Grand National winner in 1936 when the reins parted on Anthony Mildmay's mount, Davy Jones, at the penultimate fence and he ran out at the last, leaving Reynoldstown and Fulke Walwyn to win. Luckily in Devon Loch's case, his owner, trainer and jockey were all sportsmen in the finest tradition of the race and suffered their disappointment with true dignity. John Hislop, a friend of Dick's and a great amateur both on the Flat and under National Hunt Rules wrote about the incident: 'The general feeling was expressed by the cheers which greeted HM Queen Elizabeth The Queen Mother as she walked through the paddock to see her horse and jockey, who was likewise applauded as he made his sad way back on foot. There are times when defeat is greater than victory and this was one.'

Before leaving this tragic incident, I would like to quote what Dick said to me in an interview in 1992, nearly forty years after the event. I have transcribed this verbatim from the tape recording of the interview.

'I still think it was the crowd yelling and as Devon Loch approached the outside of the water jump, as you see in the film, he pricked his ears as if to say, "I was here last time round." As he did that, his hind quarters just refused to act. He brought his forefeet up to stop himself going over. Other people have said that this was to jump the fence alongside. We slid along the ground, his forefeet out and his hindfeet behind and how I didn't fall off him, I don't know. He got to his feet and if I could have got him going, we were still far enough in front to have beaten ESB, but as he got up he more or less collapsed again. His legs gave way at the back, so I had no option but to get off him. His lad then came running up to take charge of him.

'As I walked away, an ambulance drove up. The driver lowered his window and said, "Jump in the back, mate." I have never been more pleased to get in an ambulance in all my life. I sat there with the other casualties he had collected, and he drove to the First Aid Room the other side of the weighing-room where I got out. I took off my colours and was sitting there in my breeches and boots when Peter Cazalet came and sat beside me. He was as dumbfounded as I was; it was terrible for him because of the Davy Jones disaster in 1938. Peter said to me, "Come along, we have been asked to go up and see the Royal Party." The Queen, the Queen Mother and Princess Margaret – they were all there – were all flabbergasted. The Queen Mother asked what had happened and, well, I couldn't tell her. I said, "I don't know." Her reply was, "Well, that's racing." There could not have been anyone more philosophical than she.

'On the Saturday night following the National, Mary and I and the two boys were staying in the Buck Inn at Bangor-on-Dee. Edward Courage was there for the salmon fishing. The fish weren't biting at all that year and the next morning, as we were preparing to leave for Blewbury, the landlord of the hotel handed me a lovely salmon. It was the only one that Edward Courage had caught and he had given it to me because I hadn't won the Grand National. What a lovely gesture! He was the most charming man and I'm glad I won a few races for him.

'Devon Loch was a lovely horse to ride, and I had a terrific ride all the way round that National on him. Always handy, he jumped beautifully throughout and everything went right – until twenty yards from the post.'

DAILY DOUBLE			

THIRD RACE   About four miles and 856 yards   **BLUE BADGE**

3-15 The GRAND NATIONAL STEEPLE CHASE

(Handicap) of 10 sov. each, 50 sov. extra if left in after Tuesday, January 31st, with an additional 40 sov. if left in after Tuesday, March 6th, with 6000 sov. (including a trophy value 500 sov.) added; second to receive 10%, third 5%, and fourth 2½% of the whole stakes ; for six yrs old and upwards which, up to or on the day of closing, have been placed first, second, or third by the judge in a steeple chase of any distance at Aintree, Liverpool (this does not include such steeple chases run at the December Meeting on the Mildmay Course), or which have won a steeple chase of three miles or upwards of the advertised value of 300 sov., or with at least 250 sov. added to a sweepstakes (or the equivalent in foreign distances and money), or which have won any steeple chase value 400 sov. to the winner (or the equivalent in foreign money), selling races in every case excepted ; weights published January 26th at noon : the highest weight to be not more than 12st. 7lb. and the lowest weight not less than 10st ; the GRAND NATIONAL COURSE, about four miles and 856 yards.

Declaration of forfeit to Messrs. Weatherby and Sons only. 61 entries, 60 sov. forfeit declared for 9 and 10 sov. forfeit declared for 13. Closed January 3rd, 1956.

。 The trainer of the winner will receive a Cup value 50 sov. and the rider of the winner a Cup value 25 sov.

There will be a Parade for this race.

VALUE TO WINNER £8,695 5s. 0d.

Jockey			Age st. lb.	Colours	Trainer
B. Marshall	1	EARLY MIST Mr. John Dunlop 11 12	2	Green and yellow (hlvd), slvs. reversed, green cap	B. Marshall
		ch g Brumeux—Sudden Dawn			
T. Taaffe	2	ROYAL TAN Prince Aly Khan 12 12	1	Green, red sash, green cap	M. V. O'Brien (In Ireland)
		ch g Tartan—Princess of Birds			
P. Taaffe	3	QUARE TIMES Mrs. W. H. E. Welman 10 11	12	Red, white and blue hps, blue slvs, red cap	M. V. O'Brien (In Ireland)
		b g Artist's Son—Lavenco			
R. Emery	4	MARINER'S LOG	9 11 11	Black, gold slvs, red cap	G. Beeby
		The Late Ld. Bicester ch g Archive—She Gone			
R. Francis	5	DEVON LOCH Queen Elizabeth 10 11	4	Blue, buff stripes, blue slvs, black cap, gold tassel	P. Cazalet
		b or br g Devonian—Coolaleen			
F. Winter	6	SUNDEW Mrs. Geoffrey Kohn 10 11	4	Flame, emerald green sleeves, flame cuffs	F. Hudson
		ch g Sun King—Parsonstown			
D. V. Dick	7	E.S.B. Mrs. Leonard Carver 10 11	3	Green, white hoop and armlets	T. F. Rimell
		b or br g Bidar—English Summer			
A. P. Thompson	8	HIGH GUARD Mr. J. A. Keith 9 11	1	Brown, light blue slvs and cap	N. Crump
		gr g Fishguard—High Places			
H. J. East	9	MUCH OBLIGED Mr. H. Draper 8 11	0	Red and white (halved), slvs reversed, check cap	N. Crump
		bl or br g Cameron—May Sen			
Mr. R. Brewis	10	DUNBOY II Mrs. M. Bruce 12 11	0	Saxe blue and white (halved), blue collar and sleeves, quartered cap	J. S. Wight
		b g Pluxit—Gaiety			
R. Turnell	11	CAREY'S COTTAGE	9 10 13	Chocolate, yellow collar, cuffs and cap	G. Balding
		Col. W. H. Whitbread b g Uncle Willie—Halo			

Continued on next page.

Jockey			Age st. lb.	Colours	Trainer
J. Dowdeswell	12	ARMORIAL III Mme. K. Hennessy	7 10 10	Straw, chocolate hoop	F. Walwyn
		b g Souverain—Skiperai			
L. McMorrow	13	MERRY WINDSOR Mr. I. Holliday	8 10 10	Yellow, red and green quartered cap	D. Doyle
		b g Foxlight—Courcelle			
R. Morrow	14	MUST Mrs. W. L. Pilkington	8 10 10	Dark blue, light blue hoop and slvs, white cap	A. S. Kilpatrick
		b g Umidkhan—Cadamstown Lass			
T. Molony	15	KEY ROYAL Mr. A. H. Birtwistle	8 10 8	Maroon, yellow hpd slvs, check cap	W. Stephenson
		b g Royal Charger—Keyboard			
A. Freeman	16	M'AS-TU-VU Queen Elizabeth	10 10 6	Blue, buff stripes, blue slvs, white cap	P. Cazalet
		br g Pampeiro—Malle Post			
Mr. C. Pocock	17	REVEREND PRINCE Mr. P. Dufosee	10 10 5	Khaki, dark green cross belts, black cap	P. Dufosee
		b g His Reverence—Princess Pat			
P. A. Farrell	18	WITTY Mr. Clifford Nicholson 11 10	4	Grey, scarlet slvs, collar, braid and cap	W. Hall
		br g Foroughi—Brown Wings			
D. Ancil	19	DOMATA Mr. E. Stanning	10 10 4	Canary, light blue slvs, check cap	F. Cundell
		b g Domaha—Sunita			
Mr. C. Hailstone	20	POLONIUS Mrs. D. Hailstone	10 10 3	Blue, white hoop, blue sleeves and cap	G. Burnham
		ch g Epigram—Charmain			
R. J. Hamey	21	ATHENIAN Col. W. H. Whitbread	7 10 3	Chocolate, yellow collar, cuffs and cap	G. Balding
		br g The Phoenix—Felorbia			
Mr. J. Straker	22	GENTLE MOYA Mr. J. J. Straker	10 10 2	Scarlet, green hoop, white cap	C. Bewicke
		b m Steel-point—Laura Day			
C. Finnegan	23	NO RESPONSE	10 10 1	Blue, red hoop	J. Osborne (In Ireland)
		Sir Thomas Ainsworth br m Iceberg II—Water Gypsy			
J. A. Bullock	24	CLEARING Mr. M. Kingsley	9 10 1	Black and pink (qtd), pink cap	W. Stephenson
		b g Labrador—Colimene VI			
A. Oughton	25	EAGLE LODGE Mr. N. A. Mardon	7 10 0	Dark blue, two pale green diagonal stripes, and hoop on cap	M. Feakes
		b g Jamaica Inn—Mountain Side			
N. Wilkinson	26	ONTRAY Capt. Scott Briggs	8 10 0	Primrose	L. S. Briggs
		br g Legend of France—Guinea Fowl			
J. Cuddihy	27	VICTORY MORN Mr. John Dixon	12 10 0	Yellow, brown and yellow qtd cap	J. Dixon
		br g Pane Beg—Market Bar			
A. Grantham	28	WILD WISDOM Mr. E. Foster	11 10 0	Grey, Royal blue hoop on body	J. Ford
		br g Perion—Miss Fix-It			
P. Major	29	BORDER LUCK Mr. J. R. Bower	11 10 0	Gold and green (halved), nigger brown cap	J. R. Bower
		bl g Squadron Castle or Port of Call—Luck			
J. Power	30	PIPPYKIN Mr. R. D. Darragh	8 10 0	Black, scarlet slvs and cap, qtd cap	S. Parker
		ch g Escamillo—Relizane			
S. Mellor	31	MARTINIQUE Mr. A. Greenberg	10 10 0	White, green sleeves and sash, qtd cap	G. R. Owen
		b g Mieuxce—Carruse			
	32	VENETIAN LAW Mr. M. L. Marsh	9 10 0	Violet and white check, white cap	M. L. Marsh
		b m Within-the-Law—Lady Wick			
K. Maudsley	33	SUN CLASP Mr. E. O. Boardman	8 10 0	White, dark green slvs, hooped cap	K. Maudsley
		b g Sol Oriens—Buckle			

THE SPREAD OF RUNNERS FROM THE 1956 GRAND NATIONAL RACE CARD

Previous page: IN THE PARADE RING BEFORE THE 1956 GRAND NATIONAL. WITH DICK ARE HM THE QUEEN AND PRINCESS MARGARET. HM THE QUEEN MOTHER TALKS TO PETER CAZALET, DEVON LOCH'S TRAINER. ARTHUR FREEMAN IS ON THE FAR RIGHT

DEVON LOCH IS LED OUT BY JOHN HOLE

THE START OF THE RACE. THERE WERE
TWENTY-NINE RUNNERS

BECHER'S FIRST TIME. DEVON LOCH AND DICK ARE CLOSEST TO THE
CAMERA; EAGLE LODGE (A. OUGHTON) PECKS ON LANDING

DEVON LOCH LEADING ESB (DAVE DICK) OVER THE LAST FENCE

THE SEQUENCE OF THE FAMOUS SPREADEAGLE, JUST FIFTY YARDS FROM THE FINISHING POST

DICK WALKS AWAY FROM THE SCENE, A DREAM SHATTERED

DEVON LOCH IS LED BACK

CRUDWELL BEING LED IN AFTER WINNING THE WELSH GRAND NATIONAL, 1956

Incidentally, when Mrs Mirabel Topham sold Aintree Racecourse, she took a sliver of wood from the finishing post and presented it to Dick. He had it made into a paper weight and it, together with a cigarette box presented to him by Her Majesty Queen Elizabeth The Queen Mother as a memento of the Grand National he nearly won, are two of Dick's most treasured possessions.

There is no doubt that this Grand National experience would have unnerved lesser jockeys, but the following Tuesday Dick was back at work at Sandown where he won a novice chase on Never Say When, trained by Frank Cundell. On Easter Tuesday, exactly a week later, he rode a double at Chepstow on horses trained by Frank Cundell including winning the Welsh Grand National by a head on Bunny Cooper's Crudwell.

Dick's final big win of the season came on Lochroe in the Holman Cup at the Cheltenham April meeting and he finished off the season with forty-one winners. Apart from the disaster in the Grand National, 1955/56 had been a fairly good season and the next season looked like it would be even better.

Dick's first winner of any note was when Devon Loch caused a major surprise by winning a 2½-mile hurdle race at Nottingham on 29 October. His first outing since the Grand National, the race was mainly intended to get him back into racing trim. However, after the penultimate hurdle, Dick suddenly got an electric run from him and they won by two lengths. The next outing was in the Cottage Rake Chase on 29 November at Kempton when they were beaten half a length by the very useful Key Royal. Clearly Devon Loch was still an extremely able horse as, on 13 December, he beat Early Mist, winner of the 1953 Grand National, at level terms in a match in the Ewell Chase at Sandown.

Dick and Devon Loch's next race was in the King George VI Chase at Kempton. Once again, the first day was postponed to the second day whose card was abandoned. Peter Cazalet had three runners – Devon Loch who was 7/4 favourite, Lochroe, ridden by Arthur Freeman at 4/1 and Rose Park, with Michael Scudamore up, at 100/6. Rose Park, although really only a two-miler, jumped off and under an inspired ride from Michael built up an enormous lead and, although stopping fast near the line, managed to win by two lengths from Devon Loch.

Her Majesty Queen Elizabeth The Queen Mother had acquired another top-class horse in Double Star who was to win many races for her, the first two of these ridden by Dick. They won a novice hurdle on 7 December at Lingfield and eight days later completed a two-timer at Hurst Park. Lochroe started off the season by winning a handicap hurdle at Fontwell and showed he was still an improving horse by winning the Eridge Chase at Lingfield.

The New Year started well when the Queen Mother's Flamingo Bay ran above all expectations to be third in a chase on 5 January at Windsor. On the following Monday, Dick and Crudwell had their fifteenth win together at Leicester; this was to be their last appearance together – and, as it turned out, Dick's last winner. Crudwell went soldiering on, winning on his last appearance on 15 September 1960 when he and Michael Scudamore – the father of Peter – won at Wincanton.

Crudwell was indeed a great horse. He won in every year of the fifties and in the first year of the sixties. In all, he won a total of fifty races, which is still a record, seven on the flat, four over hurdles and thirty-nine over fences. Dick's record on him was twenty-two rides, of which there were fifteen wins, four times placed and only three times unplaced.

DEVON LOCH AND EARLY MIST (BRYAN MARSHALL) TOGETHER AT THE
LAST BUT ONE FENCE IN THE EWELL CHASE, SANDOWN, DECEMBER 1956

Dick says of him: 'He was a lovely horse to ride, beautifully balanced and, in many ways, very like Finnure. As soon as they landed over a fence, both would prick up their ears and one could sense them looking for the next obstacle.'

Following Crudwell's win at Leicester, Dick and Double Star ran a blinding good race to be third in a very hot novice hurdle at Hurst Park on 9 January, so when Dick drove the few miles from his Blewbury home to Newbury on Friday 11 January, the prospects for the rest of the season seemed reasonably rosy. He had already ridden twenty-two winners that season; Devon Loch had a real chance of landing the Grand National and Lochroe had a sporting outsider's chance in the Gold Cup. However, it was not to be; riding Prince Stephen in a handicap hurdle, Dick had a fall at the last but one flight and

DOUBLE STAR OUT IN THE LEAD, BUSHEY PARK NOVICES HURDLE AT
HURST PARK, JANUARY 1957

was knocked about by the runners following. Although he walked to the ambulance for a lift back to the First Aid Room and told the doctor he was sure he would be riding again the next day, Dick's injuries were very much more serious than he thought. He had broken his wrist and was badly bruised all over. Still, he hoped to be back racing again within a month or so. On 19 January, Devon Loch ran in the Mildmay Memorial Chase at Sandown ridden by Arthur Freeman. He ran well for most of the race, leading over the second last, but fell back rapidly to finish fourth. It transpired that the horse had broken down and this ended his racing days.

With his old friend Devon Loch in retirement, Dick talked things over with the present Mar-

quess of Abergavenny. Lord Abergavenny had been a successful amateur rider under National Hunt Rules in his younger days and was at that time embarking on an even more successful career as a turf administrator, which included a period as the Queen's representative at Royal Ascot.

Perhaps, however, the most outstanding feature of this charming and unassuming man was his gift of friendship. For many years his impartial and respected advice had been sought by many people in racing, including members of the Royal Family, and it therefore wasn't surprising that Dick should consult him about his own future and whether or not he should retire while he was still at the top. Dick accepted Lord

MISS NORAH WILMOTT AND DICK WITH DEVON LOCH AT BINFIELD

Abergavenny's advice to retire, so that the last winner Dick rode was on Crudwell at Leicester on 7 January 1957, while his last ride of all was four days later on Prince Stephen.

The rest, as they say, is history. Dick wrote a very successful autobiography called *The Sport of Queens* and spent the next sixteen years as a newspaper man with the *Sunday Express* as one of their racing team. Later came the formidable series of internationally bestselling thrillers – but that is not my story.

There only seems one suitable way of ending this book and that is by quoting Doug Francis on his younger brother's racing career. 'He rode quite a few winners for me. I am very proud of him as he was a remarkable jockey. He had the most beautiful hands and you never caught him in the wrong position in a race. In my opinion, of all the top jockeys I saw ride, Dick was the finest horseman of them all.'

Index